JUSTICE LEAGUE

VOLUME 1 ORIGIN

JUSTICE LEAGUE
VOLUME 1: ORIGIN

GEOFF **JOHNS** writer

JIM **LEE** penciller

SCOTT **WILLIAMS** inker

SANDRA **HOPE, BATT**
& MARK **IRWIN** additional inks

CARLOS **D'ANDA** epilogue artist

ALEX **SINCLAIR**
with GABE **ELTAEB,** TONY **AVINA** & HI-FI colorists

PATRICK **BROSSEAU** letterer

JIM **LEE,** SCOTT **WILLIAMS** & ALEX **SINCLAIR**
original series & collection cover artists

EDDIE BERGANZA BRIAN CUNNINGHAM Editors – Original Series
REX OGLE Associate Editor – Original Series DARREN SHAN Assistant Editor – Original Series
PETER HAMBOUSSI Editor ROBBIN BROSTERMAN Design Director – Books
ROBBIE BIEDERMAN Publication Design

BOB HARRAS Senior VP – Editor-in-Chief, DC Comics

DIANE NELSON President DAN DIDIO and JIM LEE Co-Publishers
GEOFF JOHNS Chief Creative Officer
JOHN ROOD Executive VP – Sales, Marketing & Business Development
AMY GENKINS Senior VP – Business & Legal Affairs NAIRI GARDINER Senior VP – Finance
JEFF BOISON VP – Publishing Planning MARK CHIARELLO VP – Art Direction & Design
JOHN CUNNINGHAM VP – Marketing TERRI CUNNINGHAM VP – Editorial Administration
ALISON GILL Senior VP – Manufacturing & Operations HANK KANALZ Senior VP – Vertigo & Integrated Publishing
JAY KOGAN VP – Business & Legal Affairs, Publishing JACK MAHAN VP – Business Affairs, Talent
NICK NAPOLITANO VP – Manufacturing Administration SUE POHJA VP – Book Sales
COURTNEY SIMMONS Senior VP – Publicity BOB WAYNE Senior VP – Sales

DC Comics, 1700 Broadway, New York, NY 10019
A Warner Bros. Entertainment Company
Printed by RR Donnelley, Salem, VA, USA. 6/14/13. Second Printing.
ISBN: 978-1-4012-3788-2

Library of Congress Cataloging-in-Publication Data

Johns, Geoff, 1973-
Justice League volume 1 : origin / Geoff Johns, Jim Lee, Scott
Williams.
p. cm.
"Originally published in single magazine form in JUSTICE LEAGUE
1-6"—T.p. verso.
ISBN 978-1-4012-3461-4 (hardcover : alk. paper)
1. Graphic novels. I. Lee, Jim, 1964- II. Williams, Scott. III.
Title.
PN6728.J87J65 2012
741.5'973—dc23
2011051844

CENTRAL CITY. CRIME LAB.

I'M RIGHT IN THE *MIDDLE* OF PROCESSING THIS CASE!

STOP *ARGUING* ALLEN, AND BOX IT UP.

NO.

NO?

THIS MAN WAS MURDERED IN THE PARKING LOT OF HIS OFFICE. IT MIGHT HAVE BEEN MADE TO *LOOK* LIKE A ROBBERY, BUT THE LOT IS *LOCKED* AFTER HOURS. WHOEVER KILLED HIM HAD *ACCESS*.

THIS CASE IS *SOLVABLE* IF WE MOVE *FAST*--

AND *FAST* IS THE WORD OF THE *WEEK*. THE CHIEF WANTS EVERYONE WORKING ON *THE FLASH CASE*, ALLEN.

EVERYONE.

ON THE *FLASH CASE*.

THAT INCLUDES *YOU*, GOLDEN BOY.

THIS MAN WAS A *HUSBAND* AND A *FATHER*, DIRECTOR SINGH.

DON'T LET HIM BECOME A *COLD CASE*.

I'M SORRY, BARRY, I REALLY AM, BUT THIS *ISN'T* MY CALL.

I WANT THE CRIME LAB TO GET BACK TO *SOLVING MURDERS* AS *BADLY* AS YOU...

..BUT WE *CAN'T* UNTIL WE FIND OUT *WHO* THE FLASH REALLY *IS*.

"TEAR GAS. SONIC GRENADES. TASERS."

I DON'T LIKE BEING ATTACKED.

HE ATTACKED ME!

YOU'RE *BOTH* CONFUSED, LANTERN.

I THINK THIS IS

A BIG

MISUNDERSTANDING.

DON'T BOTHER

TRYING TO

CATCH ME, SUPERMAN.

I'VE *NEVER* BEEN TOUCHED.

"I'M WORRIED THAT THERE'S *MORE* THAN ONE OF THESE BOXES OUT THERE."

DETROIT.
S.T.A.R. LABS--SUPER-HUMAN STUDY.

IT WAS RECOVERED FROM THE WRECKAGE OF SUPERMAN'S BATTLE EARLIER THIS MORNING.

DID IT BELONG TO SUPERMAN, SARAH?

WE DON'T THINK SO. IT'S BEEN HARD TO DETERMINE ANYTHING ABOUT IT, STARTING WITH THE *METAL* IT'S MADE OF.

HOWEVER, WE *HAVE* PICKED UP SOME KIND OF *SIGNAL* BROADCASTING FROM IT.

AND WE'VE FOUND SIMILAR BROADCASTING COMING FROM NEW ENGLAND, WASHINGTON D.C., CENTRAL CITY AND COAST CITY.

I SUPPOSE IT HASN'T GONE UNNOTICED THAT THOSE ARE ALL PLACES OF SUPER-HUMAN ACTIVITY.

NO, DR. STONE. IT'S CLEAR THAT THE SUPER-HUMANS ARE *INVOLVED* IN THIS.

DR. STONE?

YOUR SON IS HERE.

I DON'T HAVE TIME TO SEE HIM RIGHT NOW.

HE SEEMS PRETTY *UPSET.*

AGAIN.

HHFF. FOR GOD'S SAKE...

SHE BELIEVES IN ZEUS FOR GOD'S SAKE.

NEVER MIND WHAT SHE BELIEVES IN, LOOK AT WHAT SHE'S DOING! SHE'S SKEWERING PEOPLE!

THERE'VE BEEN DOZENS OF INNOCENT BYSTANDERS INJURED BECAUSE OF SUPER-HUMANS LIKE THIS AMAZON.

SHE'S SPENT HER LIFE TRAINING FOR WAR.

WHAT WAR IS SHE EVEN TALKING ABOUT?

SHE CAUSED OVER ONE HUNDRED MILLION DOLLARS IN PROPERTY DAMAGE.

SUPERMAN'S CAUSED THREE HUNDRED.

YOU'RE GOING TO HELL PAGAN

PAGANS GOT NO SOUL

SHE'S STILL WORSE THAN ANY OF THEM. SHE SWINGS THAT SWORD WITH A SMILE.

Y'KNOW FORGET ZEUS, THESE SUPER-HUMANS ARE GODS. AND THEY'RE REAL.

DIANA?!

SHE'S GONE, COLONEL TREVOR.

I CAN SEE THAT SHE'S GONE, BEN.

SHE WAS SUPPOSED TO WAIT FOR ME. WHAT HAPPENED?!

SHE WAS FLIPPING THROUGH TV CHANNELS. SHE WAS ARGUING WITH THEM...AS IF THEY COULD ACTUALLY HEAR HER.

UNTIL SHE SAW A REPORT ABOUT A WINGED MONSTER TERRORIZING PEOPLE IN DOWNTOWN D.C. THAT'S WHEN SHE TOOK OFF.

YOU'RE WORRIED ABOUT HER OUT THERE, HUH?

I'M WORRIED ABOUT EVERYONE ELSE! DIANA'S ALWAYS LOOKING FOR A FIGHT!

AND SHE ALWAYS FINDS ONE.

WHY DIDN'T YOU STOP HER?

YOU'RE KIDDING, RIGHT?

ORR

THIS IS JUDGMENT DAY!

I GET RADIO BROADCASTS IN MY EARPIECE AND THIS *ISN'T* AN *ISOLATED* INCIDENT. THIS IS HAPPENING ACROSS THE WORLD, GUYS.

WHAT *ELSE* IS NEW, FLASH?

CONCENTRATE, LANTERN! THE THINGS YOU MAKE WITH THAT RING ARE *BREAKING* APART. THAT MEANS YOUR MIND IS *SCATTERED*, RIGHT?

YOU NEED TO CALM DOWN AND--

I AM CALM, *BATMAN*. I'M *ALWAYS* CALM.

THAT'S NOT WHAT IT LOOKS LIKE.

HEY, WORRY ABOUT YOURSELF. *YOU'RE* THE ONE *WITHOUT* POWERS!

SKREEEEEEE

UH... GUYS?

ANYONE ELSE *AWAKE* YET? I'M NOT THAT GOOD AT MAKING *CHITCHAT.*

FLASH?

I'M UP.

BUT NOT TO TALK.

VZZZEEOOO

SUPERMAN!

ARRGHH!

PERRKK

WHERE... WHERE ARE YOU GOING?

AHH... LANTERN.

Every civilization throughout history has had higher beings they aspire to.

I SHOULDN'T BE UP HERE.

SURE YOU SHOULD. BE PROUD.

"YOUR DAD LOOKS LIKE HE IS."

WE WERE ATTACKED BY AN *ENEMY* UNLIKE ANY WE HAVE EVER ENCOUNTERED...

...AND WE WERE SAVED BY A *TEAM* OF *HEROES* UNLIKE ANY MANKIND HAS EVER KNOWN.

CAN YOU BELIEVE THIS?

THAT THE PEOPLE AREN'T AFRAID OF US?

They are beings of great power and morality.

THAT EVERYONE THINKS WE'RE A *TEAM*. WE'RE *NOT* A TEAM.

TODAY MARKS A MOMENTOUS DAY IN HUMAN HISTORY.

IN OUR DARKEST HOUR, THESE PEOPLE DONNED THEIR *COLORFUL COSTUMES* AND WENT INTO ACTION.

COSTUMES? I DON'T WEAR A *COSTUME*. THIS IS MY *UNIFORM*.

AND THIS IS *ATLANTEAN SCALE MAIL*. DO THEY THINK I'D *CHOOSE* ORANGE?

I DON'T MIND THE ORANGE MYSELF, BUT THAT NECKLACE HAS GOTTA GO.

...THESE FRIENDS USED THEIR SUPER-POWERS TO PROTECT US...

THE SUPER-FRIENDS SAVED US, DADDY!

Beings to help us strive for better.

AND WE'RE NOT *FRIENDS* EITHER.

WE NEED TO LET THEM *THINK* WE'RE BOTH.

WHY?

IT'LL KEEP THE GOTHAM P.D. OFF MY BACK. THE AIR FORCE OFF YOURS.

I DON'T HAVE TIME TO *BELONG* TO A TEAM. I'VE GOT *OTHER* RESPONSIBILITIES.

SO DO I.

I HAVE A WHOLE *UNIVERSE* TO PROTECT.

WE CAN DO IT *TOGETHER*, GUYS.

CAN *YOU* FLY INTO SPACE?

I CAN.

THAT'S NOT THE POINT. WE ALL HAVE *OTHER* THINGS WE NEED TO DO. WE'RE *NOT* FRIENDS. WE'RE *NOT* A TEAM. THIS WAS JUST A *ONE-TIME THING*, OKAY?

YOU USED TO
LOOK AWAY FROM
EVERYTHING.

VARIANT COVER GALLERY

JUSTICE LEAGUE 1
by David Finch, Richard Friend & Peter Steigerwald

JUSTICE LEAGUE 2
by Ivan Reis, Andy Lanning & Rod Reis

JUSTICE LEAGUE 3
by Greg Capullo, Jonathan Glapion & FCO Plascencia

JUSTICE LEAGUE 4
by Andy Kubert & Alex Sinclair

JUSTICE LEAGUE 5
by Eric Basaldua & Nei Ruffino

JUSTICE LEAGUE 6
by Ivan Reis, Joe Prado & Rod Reis

JUSTICE LEAGUE 1 (second printing)
by Jim Lee, Scott Williams & Alex Sinclair

JUSTICE LEAGUE 1 (third printing)
by Jim Lee, Scott Williams & Alex Sinclair

THE STAGES OF A COVER:

1. From a first sketch by Jim Lee.
2. To tight pencils by Jim.
3. Masterly inks by longtime Jim Lee collaborator Scott Williams.
4. Finished off by the rich and lush colors of Alex Sinclair.

U.S.A.F.

XD-4224

CONFIDENTIAL
INFORMATION

> TRANSCRIPT OF INTERVIEW WITH CAPTAIN
> STEVE TREVOR, U.S.A.F. — PROJECT:
> FLIGHT TO PARADISE
>
> TRANSCRIBED BY GEOFF JOHNS

1) ENTER ON FORM 997 YOUR NAME AND DATE YOU HAD
ACCESS TO THE DOCUMENT(S).

2) EXERCISE THE NECESSARY SAFEGUARDS TO PREVENT
UNAUTHORIZED DISCLOSURE BY NEVER LEAVING THE
DOCUMENT(S) UNATTENDED EXCEPT WHEN PROPERLY
SECURED IN A LOCKED SAFE.

3) TRANSFER THE DOCUMENT(S) ONLY TO PERSONS WHO
NEED TO KNOW AND WHO POSSESS THE REQUIRED
SECURITY CLEARANCE.

4) OBTAIN A RECEIPT WHENEVER RELINQUISHING CONTROL
OF THE DOCUMENTS.

WARNING: SPECIAL ACCESS REQUIRED

CONFIDENTIAL INFORMATION

TREVOR: I already answered that, Agent Waller.

WALLER: Yes, but I still find it hard to believe that a decorated pilot in the U.S. Air Force, one of the American "heroes" who took part in Operation: Pandora's Box and survived, an expert in search and rescue who saved over twenty-three lost ships, some the size of a rowboat --

TREVOR: For the record, I've never failed a rescue.

WALLER: Yet you couldn't point on a map and give us the location of the island you crashed on. And you have no idea how to return.

TREVOR: You want to know how I got there, ask the people who sent me into that storm.

WALLER: You were sent looking for a missing U.S. Coast Guard ship.

TREVOR: Except there was no missing boat.

WALLER: There was no missing boat?

TREVOR: I checked the records when I got back. There was no missing boat. It was a lie.

WALLER: Your superior officer lied to you?

TREVOR: More likely someone lied to them. They sent me into the eye of that hurricane knowing --

WALLER: Knowing you'd "fly through a circle of golden light and crash on an island full of Amazons"? That's a direct quote from your written account.

TREVOR: That's what happened.

WALLER: What also happened is that the missing Coast Guard ship was never found, and the crew was declared lost at sea.

TREVOR: There was no ship.

WALLER: Tell that to the grieving families, Captain Trevor. And I guess we should note here you have failed a rescue. For the record. How does that feel? To fail someone?

TREVOR: Are you a psychiatrist or a government bogeyman?

WALLER: A bit of both.

WALLER: Can Wonder Woman take us to the island?

TREVOR: She wouldn't, even if she could.

WALLER: That's unacceptable.

TREVOR: She can't get home. Look, they're not a problem. She's not.

WALLER: Try telling that to the rest of the world. After what Wonder Woman did to that kidnapper --

TREVOR: He was going to kill those children.

WALLER: She slit his throat with her sword. Right in front of those kids. Is that what Amazons do? Kill unarmed men?

TREVOR: He wasn't unarmed.

WALLER: But she is an Amazon. And there are more.

TREVOR: Yes.

WALLER: What do they want?

TREVOR: They want to be left alone.

WALLER: And what does Wonder Woman want? What motivated her to come here? Why does she have no interest in even trying to go home?

TREVOR: If you have any questions, let me ask her. She'll talk to me. Just don't provoke her.

WALLER: Provoking people lets me see what they're capable of. That's my job.

TREVOR: She's only doing what she was raised to do.

WALLER: Which is?

TREVOR: Fight.

WALLER: Is your relationship romantic?

TREVOR: What? No.

WALLER: That question makes you uncomfortable.

TREVOR: Nothing makes me uncomfortable.

WALLER: I don't believe that, and neither do you. Do you believe in U.F.O.'s?

TREVOR: Do I believe in U.F.O.'s? What's that have to do with anything?

WALLER: Humor me. Do you believe in U.F.O.'s?

TREVOR: They're saying Superman's an alien, right? I guess.

WALLER: And Atlantis? Do you believe in Atlantis? A new super-human, the one they're calling Aquaman, says it exists.

TREVOR: Aquaman? The guy who talks to fish?

WALLER: And there are these strange reports from several men and women across the world. People with absolutely no connection to one another who claim to have been abducted by a wizard and tested. Tested to see if they were worthy of something called "Shazam." They're calling them magical abductees.

TREVOR: Why are you telling me all this?

WALLER: I'm making a point here, Captain Trevor. In this world of super-humans, nothing can be counted out. Nothing can be trusted. Myth is fact. Rumor is nonfiction. Things like Amazons exist.

TREVOR: Tell me something I and everyone else on this planet doesn't know.

WALLER: No one's prepared for what's coming next. It's as if everything David Graves wrote has come true.

TREVOR: Who's David Graves?

WALLER: The author of a dozen books on the mysteries of the world. You should read more, Captain Trevor. Now let's move on. Tell me about this lasso.

THE SECRET HISTORY OF

ATLANTIS

BY DAVID GRAVES

▸ HISTORIC PUBLICATIONS ◂

THE SECRET HISTORY
OF ATLANTIS

GRAVES, DAVID

HISTORIC PUBLICATIONS

ABOUT THE AUTHOR

DAVID GRAVES is the best selling world-renowned writer of some of the most popular books on the paranormal, supernatural and mythical, but he became the most important author of our time when he wrote his firsthand account of the formation of the Justice League and their role in saving him and his family. It is with great pride that Historic Publications rereleases Graves' line of World-Mystery ™ books in conjunction with the release of *THE JUSTICE LEAGUE: GODS AMONG US.*

Available at bookstores and e-book sellers everywhere:

THE YONAGUNI PYRAMID: CIVILIZATION UNKNOWN (1999)

STONEHENGE DECODED (2000)

THE SECRET HISTORY OF ATLANTIS (2002)

THE FATIMA PROPHECIES (2002)

ENTERING THE KALIASA CAVES (2003)

THE NEW SEVEN WONDERS OF THE WORLD (2004)

THE BELMEZ FACES AND BEYOND (2005)

THE TRUTH BEHIND THE TUNGUSKA EVENT (2005)

THE JUSTICE LEAGUE: GODS AMONG US (2006)

DEDICATION

David would like to dedicate this new edition of
THE SECRET HISTORY OF ATLANTIS
to his best friend and wife, Jennifer, his son, Jason,
and his ever-imaginative daughter, Emma.

He loves them more than *any* world mystery.

FOREWORD

How powerful is a story? That all depends on the author.

There's one reason that people believe Atlantis was real. Plato wrote about it. In times long before ours, Atlantis was commonly thought nothing more than a myth, a warning that no empire will last forever. It's only recently that Plato's tale of Atlantis began to be believed. Plato's name validated everything he wrote. But should we believe everything we read from Plato? Do we think an entire continent, home to a utopian society and ultimately a violent empire, was destroyed and washed away in but a day? Did Atlantis sink into the ocean to be forever lost? Are Plato's words fact or fiction?

I believe fact. I believe Atlantis was real. And I believe it still exists in some form today. And I believe after you read this book, you'll feel the same way.

I've gathered together historical accounts from the first travelers to the New World and the pirates that plagued them of encounters with aquatic humanoids who rose from the oceans and vanished just as quickly. I've spoken to Dr. Stephen Shin, the famed oceanographer and marine biologist who spent his life searching the seas for signs of the lost empire and even claims there's an Atlantean now living among us. I've traveled across the world myself to take part in Dane Dorrance's expeditions to the deep, uncovering what I believe are the remains of a path to the central city of Atlantis on the ocean floor.

The evidence is here. Believe.

David Graves
April 13, 2002

WRITTEN BY GEOFF JOHNS · DESIGN BY BRIAN WALTERS

A NEW WORLD ORDER

At the center of DC COMICS—The New 52 is the JUSTICE LEAGUE, and in the way that Geoff Johns had to structure a story that would reintroduce the World's Greatest Heroes, Jim Lee had to establish the look that would set the tone for what would be a younger and more contemporary set of heroes.

WONDER WOMAN: There was much debate on Princess Diana's legwear. This one denotes some deadly accessories.

AQUAMAN: A more crustacean-looking armor was considered but ultimately deemed to be too detailed and "crusty" a look for the regal, majestic King of the Seven Seas. Maybe an Atlantean foot soldier will carry this mantle...

EMPLOYEE DOSSIER
RESTRICTED ACCESS
FILE FORM 778M REQ

COMPILED BY
GEOFF JOHNS

DESIGNER/ARCHIVIST

ARAM R. ISAACS

DR. SILAS STONE

OCCUPATION:
Project Director: The Red Room

AGE: 42
HEIGHT: 5' 9"
WEIGHT: 155 lbs.
EYES: Brown
HAIR: Black/graying

BACKGROUND:
Dr. Silas Stone graduated top of his class from the University of Michigan in Synthetic Biology and Technical Cybernetics. Although heavily pursued by LexCorp, Stone was recruited by S.T.A.R. Labs to participate in the recovery of ███████████. Stone was the team leader in the successful reverse engineering of ███████████████. Although replication of ████████ has so far failed, the technology involved led to the creation of promethium. With promethium, Stone established the Red Room: a level nine S.T.A.R. Labs facility in Detroit built to collect and analyze foreign, extraterrestrial and sentient technology deemed too dangerous to share with the world.

The death of Dr. Stone's wife, Dr. Elinore Stone, remains clouded by controversy. Although not held responsible legally, Stone continues to blame himself for her death. Thorough investigation confirmed that no one was at fault and that no one could have saved her. Stone is not convinced.

DR. THOMAS MORROW

OCCUPATION:
Project Manager: The Red Room

AGE: 31
HEIGHT: 5' 11"
WEIGHT: 187 lbs.
EYES: Blue
HAIR: Black

BACKGROUND:
Dr. Thomas Morrow earned master degrees in Emerging Technologies, Strategic Foresight and Future Studies from Harvard University. From a young age, Morrow exhibited a strong interest in future technology, citing influence from science fiction, specifically the works of H.G. Wells. Originally Morrow dedicated himself to the study of the possibility of time travel, but he abandoned it after an accident in particular FTL (faster-than-light) travel nearly took his own life and that of his former colleague Dr. Will Magnus. This event resulted in the resignation of Will Magnus who now works for the U.S. military on an unknown program called Project: Metal Men.

After his recovery, Morrow was recruited by Dr. Silas Stone to assist in the establishment of the Red Room located in the S.T.A.R. Labs facility in Detroit, Michigan.

There has been some criticism leveled at Morrow recently. Complaints have been filed for his lack of transparency on his projects and his sarcastic and demeaning attitude towards his fellow scientists, save for Dr. Stone. Additionally, Morrow is under investigation by the F.B.I. for reasons that are unclear.

SARAH CHARLES

OCCUPATION:
Intern

AGE: 17
HEIGHT: 5' 5"
WEIGHT: 112 lbs.
EYES: Brown
HAIR: Black

BACKGROUND:
Sarah Charles applied to the S.T.A.R. Labs internship program while studying for her master's degrees at the University of Michigan. Her father Daniel Charles is the current C.C.O. of Motor City Automotive while her mother is Congress-woman Sasha Charles representing Michigan's 9th District. Although Sarah Charles was moved to the top of the list because of her parents' involvement in the support of S.T.A.R Labs, Dr. Stone maintains that her credentials made her the prime candidate regardless.

Charles skipped several grades at a very young age, showing an intelligence level and learning capacity far beyond the other children around her. Charles graduated from Marion High School in Bloomfield Hills, Michigan at the age of 15. She received numerous awards for her scientific papers and projects, most notably her thesis on cyberware and its potential emotional impact on society.

Despite her parents' initial encouragement of Charles' internship at S.T.A.R. Labs, they have requested she end the program early because of the changing political climate and the recent controversies surrounding the existence of S.T.A.R. Labs and its shifting focus to the study of super-human biology and technology. With her 18th birthday weeks away, that decision will soon rest in Charles' hands. We expect her to not only remain at S.T.A.R. Labs, but to soon become an integral part of the team overseeing the Red Room.

PROF. ANTHONY IVO

OCCUPATION:
Project Director: A-Maze Operating System

AGE: 37
HEIGHT: 5' 10"
WEIGHT: 185 lbs.
EYES: Blue
HAIR: Black

BACKGROUND:
Professor Anthony Ivo served as head of the Cellular and Structural Biology department at Ivy University for over a decade until he was recruited by Dr. Silas Stone to oversee the biotechnology efforts of S.T.A.R. Labs. Professor Ivo has pioneered the organic pattern process: the means of creating technology to mimic organic life down to the cellular level. Although Ivo has had great success in developing the A-Maze Operating System that mimics cellular regeneration in trial tests with mice, he remains one of the most unpredictable members of Dr. Stone's team. Ivo has been known to disappear for days at a time, often consumed by his own personal projects which have been consistently frowned upon by S.T.A.R. Labs. Consequently, a parallel support program based on Ivo's designs, the B-Maze Operating System, was built without his knowledge. It has, thus far, showed results comparable to those of A-Maze OS.

Ivo suffers from thanatophobia: a fear of death. This often manifests in panic attacks and drug use and has led to several confrontations with Ivo's fellow team members.

Stone is currently looking to replace Ivo, calling him "a bomb waiting to go off."

Concept art by Cully Hamner
Based on designs by Jim Lee

Character Chest Emblem

Costume Details & Call-outs

Glove Details: Three recessed louver-like shapes are located on both topside and palm side of gloves. Gloves are a dense but malleable leather with ribbing on fingers (palm side), raised piping and convex metal knuckles (topside). Mesh detail appears just beneath the palm and inside the louver shapes. The fins can be released from gloves and are made of a razor-sharp, beveled metal that can penetrate solid rock surfaces. They are only used to assist Batman in his crimefigthing but never to maim or kill.

Boot Detail: Recessed louver-like detail on both sides of calves; Beveled knee pads in shape of bat heads are gray.

Convex metal ampules form belt and contain many of Batman's secret and useful gadgets. The buckle is made up of beveled metal platelets.

Character Name: Batman
Real Name: Bruce Wayne
Height: 6' 2"
Weight: 210 lbs

Eye Color on Cowl: White
First Appearance:
Batman: Justice League #1 (2011)

NOTE:
When applying Bat Emblem to a 3D figure, ensure that it conforms to the curve of Batman's chest area as shown in the artwork.

Cape is made of a durable, lightweight leather fabric that aerodynamically supports Batman with short gliding capability.

Back of belt is an intricate containment device and can be detached to be used as a tool.

Recessed Detail

Recessed louver detail with mesh interior back of boots. Raised leather surface conforms to the shape of the calves and ends in an angled point.

Front

Back

Head & Neck Details
Cowl is completely black when sculpted (3D).

Concept art by Cully Hamner
Based on designs by Jim Lee

Character Chest Emblem

Early sketch by Jim Lee

SUPERMAN: The red underwear is gone, and in this version the cape is directly attached to the armor itself. The full story of this costume will be played out in ACTION COMICS.

Costume Details & Call-outs

Sleeve Detail: Elaborate recessed detail runs along the arm and other areas of costume. Piping on sleeve should be red (see inset).

Boot Detail: Five horizontal seams at sides; raised piping at center and along edges.

Recessed areas of belt (buckle and on strap) should be beveled on 3D product.

Character Name: Superman
Real Name: Kal-El
AKA: Clark Kent
Height: 6' 3"
Weight: 235 lbs

Eye Color: Blue
Hair Color: Black
First Appearance: Justice League #1 (2011)

When applying S-Shield to a 3D figure, ensure that it conforms to the curve of Superman's chest area as shown in the artwork.

Collar has red piping.

S-Shield on back of cape is black outline against red.

Recessed Detail

Base of cape comes to a point at center.

Head & Neck Details
Hair should be completely black when sculpted (3D).

Early sketch by Jim Lee

Character Chest Emblem

Concept art by Cully Hamner

Based on designs by Jim Lee

Note that on costume, the ring surrounding the emblem is the same thickness as the emblem.

Costume Details & Call-Outs

Ring: Negative area in the center of the ring glows continuously and more intensely when active.

Boots: Hal's boots are made of a soft, lightweight leathery material and feature rubber sneaker-like soles.

GREEN LANTERN: Here's an earlier, far more complicated version of the suit that was rejected earlier on. Design elements made their way into other non-Justice League characters.

Chest Area: The chest emblem on Green Lantern's costume glows continuously even when inactive. It radiates a green plasma-like energy when active or engaging in combat. The lines running through the upper shoulders and the chest also glow like the emblem although with slightly less intensity since there is less surface area. The linear detail maintains a faint glow when Hal's powers are inactive.

Character Name: Green Lantern
Real Name: Hal Jordan
Height: 6' 2"
Weight: 186 lbs.

Eye Color: Brown
Hair Color: Brown
First Appearance:
Justice League #1 (2011)

Recessed areas of costume glow with the same energy emitted from Hal's ring and chest emblem.

White gloves.

Boots are made of a lightweight leathery material.

Sneaker-like rubber soles with "air-cushion" portion on heel.

Hair is tousled with a few loose strands cascading over the forehead.

High mandarin collar

Costume Details & Call-outs

Pulsating LED power gauge

Sonic Canon Disruptor (Standby): The robotic arm is synced with Cyborg's nervous system. It generates and releases intense high-pressured sonic blasts and frequencies.

Sonic Canon Disruptor (Active): When active, the canon opens and releases concentric blasts.

Cyborg has the ability to transform parts of his robotics into technologically-advanced tools and weapons.

Hands are made of a refined kevlar material that providing a vise-like grip and durability.

Character Name: Cyborg
Real Name: Victor Stone
Height: 6' 5"
Weight: 385 lbs

Eye Color: Brown
Hair Color: Black
First Appearance: Justice League #1 (2011)

NOTE:
Cyborg's robotic body has a chrome finish with a slightly recessed black metal over his pecs and shoulder blades. The ribbed detail along the sides of his body, inner thighs, calves and hands are a gun-metal grey color.

In standby mode, Cyborg's human flesh is visible on upper arms. With the exception of 3/4 of his head and upper arms, Cyborg's body is covered by a titanium alloy and carbon-fiber composite.

When activated, this 3-dimensional fork-like device projects outward and downward to form another one of Cyborg's powerful weapons.

Metal plates are pieced together to form the boots and other areas of the body.

Ribbed metal detail provides an additional layer of protection and allows for ease of movement.

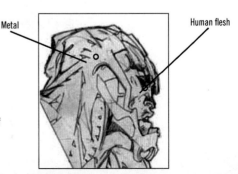

Metal

Human flesh

Recessed detail supported by two metal cylindrical pins. Soles of boots have metal treads.

Concept art by Francis Manapul
Based on designs by Jim Lee

Character Chest Emblem

Electric Seams
When running at super speed, the black seams of The Flash's costume light up and pulse with electricity. When standing still or walking, the seams remain as black linear detail and do not light up.

Back of Belt
The back of the belt differs from the front in that a narrow V-shape is created where the lightning bolts meet.

Character Name: The Flash
Real Name: Barry Allen
Height: 5' 11"
Weight: 179 lbs.

Eye Color: Blue
First Appearance:
Justice League #1
(cover 2011)